Teaching for Authentic Intellectual Work:

Standards and Scoring Criteria

for Teachers' Tasks, Student Performance, and Instruction

Fred M. Newmann, M. Bruce King, Dana L. Carmichael

THE CENTER FOR
Authentic Intellectual Work

The standards, criteria, and scoring rules for authentic intellectual work presented here are modified versions of those used in several research studies and scoring manuals published from 1995–2007, based on projects supported by the Center on Organization and Restructuring of Schools and the Research Institute on Secondary Education Reform (RISER) for Youth with Disabilities (both at the Wisconsin Center for Education Research, University of Wisconsin, Madison), and the Consortium on Chicago School Research (Annenberg Research Project), University of Chicago. References are available in Newmann, F.M., King, M.B., & Carmichael, D.L. (2007). *Authentic Instruction and Assessment: Common Standards for Rigor and Relevance in Teaching Academic Subjects.* Des Moines, IA: Iowa Department of Education. www.thedlcteam.com.

Our thanks to the staff of Teaching and Learning Services, Iowa Department of Education, for initiating the project on Authentic Intellectual Work (AIW) in Iowa high schools and for their continued support. Special thanks go to teachers, administrators, and coaches at the Iowa high schools who are implementing AIW and who provided feedback on an earlier version of this manual.

FMN, MBK, DLC

ISBN: 978-1-934690-11-6

Distributed by Itasca Books

Tasora Books
3501 Highway 100 South
Suite 220
Minneapolis, MN 55416
(952) 345-4488

Contents

The Purpose and Uses of Scoring

Research from 1990–2003 showed that teaching Language Arts, Mathematics, Science, and Social Studies in elementary, middle, and high schools nationwide which reflected the standards, criteria, and scoring rules in the AIW framework enhanced students' authentic intellectual performance. The research, however, did not evaluate the impact of programs deliberately trying to implement the AIW framework; instead, it used the standards, criteria, and scoring rules only as research tools to measure the quality of teachers' tasks, instruction, and student performance. The results of the research have led some schools, districts, and, most recently, the state of Iowa to design professional development to help teachers use the AIW framework; that is, explicitly to collaboratively plan and evaluate their teaching and student work according to these standards, criteria, and scoring rules.

Helping students produce authentic intellectual work (AIW) requires teachers to think carefully about the kinds of intellectual work they promote in their assignments, in their ways of evaluating student performance, and in how they teach lessons. This manual is intended to help teachers score their assignments, students' work, and their lessons according to the standards. To the extent that teachers strive for high scores on the standards, they are more likely to promote authentic intellectual work by students. Scoring should not be used to evaluate some teachers as "better" than others, but to help all teachers within schools, grade levels, and disciplines arrive at common, agreed-upon understandings of the standards they work toward in the tasks they assign students, in their evaluation of student performance, and in the lessons they teach.

The main point of scoring is to help teachers reflect upon and define more explicitly criteria for construction of knowledge, disciplined inquiry, and value beyond school, not to have them mechanistically adopt the precise language of each scoring rule. The standards are more likely to be used effectively when discussed and applied collaboratively with colleagues, although some teachers may prefer to implement the standards without much collegial interaction. To develop common understanding of the meaning of the standards, teachers should try to reach agreement on scores. At the same time, disagreement over scores can be very helpful; for example, when the dialogue clarifies teachers' differing intellectual priorities among the standards (e.g., when deep knowledge in a subject or lesson may be considered more important than value beyond school), or when it leads groups of teachers to change the wording of a scoring rule to facilitate agreement in scoring within a subject or grade level. In short, scoring should be undertaken not to insure that complete agreement is always reached between different scores, but as a process of helping teachers to arrive at common standards and to improve their practice according to these standards.

When teachers convene in groups to score and discuss scores, it is usually helpful to follow these guidelines: (1) Score and discuss a task, sample of work, or lesson one standard at a time; (2) Each individual should privately record an initial score; (3) The scores should then be reported and discussed within the group (4) The group discussion should focus on the specific evidence in the task, student work, or lesson that led each individual to assign their score, and how that evidence is relevant to the precise wording of the standard, criteria, and scoring rules; (5) Reaching consensus on a score is desirable, but the more important goal of group discussion is for each teacher to understand and weigh the reasons given for each score in relation to evidence in the item scored, the language of the manual, and the teacher's values.

Teachers using the standards, criteria, and scoring rules have found that the scoring and discussion process can reduce faculty conflicts based on allegiances to different "best practices," and divisions between teachers of Advanced Placement classes and teachers who teach "lower-track" classes or between more and less experienced teachers. In this sense, scoring helps to promote professional community within a school. This work also helps to improve departmental and schoolwide coherence.

The AIW framework focuses on only one aspect of instruction: authentic intellectual quality. As such, it does not address many other issues important to teachers. A broader, more complete look at the quality of instruction would probably also include other concerns such as what specific curriculum content to include, how to achieve coherence among daily lessons that connect to a larger unit of study and to other grade levels, and how to generate a positive learning climate in classrooms. Such concerns, while legitimate, can often override attention to intellectual quality. Our purpose here is to support a systematic focus on intellectual rigor and relevance, as defined by criteria for authentic intellectual work, and to help teachers apply these standards to whatever content and skills they teach.

Part I
Scoring Teachers' Tasks

Introduction and General Rules for Scoring Teachers' Tasks

A task is an assignment or assessment activity given in class or as homework. Teachers' expectations for intellectual work are revealed in instructions that tell students what they should do and that indicate what is required or expected of them to complete the task successfully. When the teacher's instructions for a task are written, or recorded in some other way, the task can be examined by colleagues, scored, and discussed to help teachers become more aware of how their tasks may or may not promote authentic intellectual work and how their tasks might be improved.

This manual presents standards, criteria, and rules for scoring tasks in Language Arts, Mathematics, Science, Social Studies, and other subjects that teachers may specify. Specific scoring rules will vary somewhat among the subjects, but applying the following **general rules** will assist in scoring tasks and reaching agreement on scores for all four subjects.

1. **Grade Level Expectations.** In scoring the level of AIW demanded in a task, take into account what students can reasonably be expected to do at the grade level.

2. **Different Parts and Dominant Expectations.** If a task has different parts with different expectations (e.g., fact-based multiple choice questions, short answer questions asking for interpretation, and a question asking students to explain their own conclusions in an essay), the overall score should reflect the apparent dominant expectations of the task.

Dominant expectations can be inferred by the proportion of **time and/or effort** that students are likely to spend on each part of a task. Dominant expectations can also be inferred if explicit criteria for evaluating student responses are stated by the teacher; for example, if questions 1–3 count 1 point each and question 4 counts 5 points, then the expectations in question 4 would be the dominant expectations.

> **Expectations can be considered "dominant" when they require 60%–100% of the time or effort students devote to a task (or equivalent weight in the teacher's evaluation criteria).**
>
> **"Some" expectation would be indicated by expectations that require about 25%–60% of students' time or effort.**
>
> **"Very little or no" expectation is defined as requiring less than 25% of students' time or effort.**

3. **Choosing between Two Close Scores.** When it is difficult to decide between two adjacent scores (3 v. 2 or 2 v. 1), use the following rules:

   a) If the specific wording of the criteria is not helpful in choosing between two scores, base the score on the general intent or **spirit** of the standard described in the introductory paragraphs of the standard and summarized for each standard below.

   Construction of Knowledge: Does the task ask students to work with knowledge to create generalizations, applications, or interpretations, or does it ask students to reproduce knowledge as it has been given to them?

   Elaborated Communication: Does the task ask students for complex and coherent clarifications, explanations, or arguments, or does it ask for brief, few-word responses?

   Value Beyond School: Does the task ask students to apply academic knowledge to understand situations and solve problems outside of school, or does it ask students to show academic knowledge only in forms useful to succeed in school?

   b) Consider the criteria to constitute the *minimum* criteria for each score. Give the higher score only when a persuasive case can be made that the minimum conditions of the higher score have been met. If not, assign the lower score.

4. **Written and Non-Written Work.** Not all tasks assigned by teachers require written work, and non-written work may demand AIW through oral expression, art, or other media. However, written student work is valuable, not only for its importance in the world beyond school, but also because it offers a convenient medium for teachers to collectively discuss and evaluate the quality of student work.

If the task requires writing, the accompanying student work should be scored on standards for student performance in the relevant discipline. Student writing can also be scored in terms of correct grammar, mechanics, sentence structure, and word choice most commonly used in Language Arts. On page 70, we provide a scoring rubric to assess these features. In addition to the discipline-based AIW standards for student written work, this standard for conventions and usage in writing can further assess the quality of student writing in any discipline.

Standards and Scoring Criteria for Language Arts Tasks

Standard 1: Construction of Knowledge In Language Arts

The task asks students to organize, interpret, analyze, synthesize, or evaluate information in addressing Language Arts concepts, themes, theories, or issues, rather than to retrieve or report information as previously given, or to repeatedly apply previously learned information, definitions, rules, and procedures.

Demands for any **ONE** of these cognitive operations (organize, interpret, analyze, synthesize, and evaluate information) signifies an expectation of construction of knowledge because each is a departure from reproducing information as is customary in tasks that ask students only to state previously learned information, definitions, rules, and procedures.

Possible indicators of demands for organizing Language Arts information include asking students to compare literary elements in a variety of texts (i.e., fiction, nonfiction, film), draw conclusions based on textual details and experience, synthesize information from multiple sources, or create originals works (i.e., fiction, nonfiction, poetry).

Possible indicators of Language Arts interpretation, synthesis, and evaluation include asking students to organize and produce various types of writing (i.e., persuasive, narrative, expository, creative), to consider alternative interpretations of literary texts, to describe an author's use of literary elements within a text, or to use research from a variety of sources to draw conclusions.

A task can be judged to make these demands of students either through explicit written instructions from the teacher (e.g., "How does Bradbury use symbol and imagery to develop theme in *Fahrenheit 451*? Use details from the story to support your answer") or, if instructions are vague, by inferring that the task, even without explicit instructions to organize, interpret, analyze, synthesize, or evaluate information, could be successfully completed **only if** students created a new interpretation or understanding, and not by reproducing an interpretation that they had been given.

SCORE	CRITERIA	NOTES
3	The task's **dominant expectation** is for students to organize, interpret, analyze, synthesize, or evaluate information about Language Arts concepts, themes, theories, or issues rather than merely to reproduce information.	60 – 100% of the time or effort (S) devote to a task
2	There is **some expectation** for students to organize, interpret, analyze, synthesize, or evaluate information about Language Arts concepts, themes, theories, or issues rather than merely to reproduce information.	25 – 60% of (S) time or effort
1	There is **very little or no expectation** for students to organize, interpret, analyze, synthesize, or evaluate information about Language Arts concepts, themes, theories, or issues. The dominant expectation is for students to retrieve or reproduce knowledge or understanding that was previously learned.	less than 25% of (S) time or effort

Standard 2: Elaborated Communication in Language Arts

The task asks students to express a conclusion or conclusions about Language Arts concepts, literary themes, theories, or issues **AND** to support their conclusions through coherent explanation or reasoning that involves elaborated use of language (written, oral, or other forms of visual/auditory expression), rather than brief declarations.

Through this type of elaborated communication, students are asked to demonstrate understanding of important Language Arts concepts, themes, theories, or issues. A task that asks for extensive factual or content knowledge alone does not ask for understanding expressed through explanations and supported conclusions.

SCORE	CRITERIA	NOTES
3	**Full elaboration:** The task asks students to express conclusions about Language Arts concepts, literary themes, theories, or issues (AND) to support their conclusions through coherent explanation or reasoning that involves elaborated use of language rather than brief declarations.	
2	**Some elaboration:** The task asks students either to express conclusions about Language Arts concepts, literary themes, theories, or issues (OR) to offer examples, illustrations, details, or reasons, but not both. The task does not clearly call for both a conclusion and an explanation, reasoning, or details that coherently support the conclusion.	
1	**Little to no elaboration:** The task asks students for very little or no elaborated communication of Language Arts concepts, literary themes, theories, or issues. The dominant expectation is for short declarative statements, fill-in-the blank, multiple choice, or true-false responses.	

Standard 3: Value Beyond School in Language Arts

The task asks students to use a Language Arts concept, literary theme, theory, or issue to clarify, represent, understand, or resolve situations in the world beyond school.

Consider the extent to which students are asked to apply a literary concept, theme, theory, or issue, not whether the content or problem posed seems "relevant" to student interests. While "relevance" can increase student engagement, relevance alone doesn't necessarily require student understanding of how Language Arts knowledge applies to situations and problems in the real world.

For example, suppose students had studied fiction or historical literature that demonstrated themes of "hero" and "victim." The task asks students to apply these themes to describe how someone they know, or a public figure they know about, might embody these themes. Such a task asks students to use Language Arts themes to better understand the world beyond school and helps students understand how academic learning relates to the real world. Tasks scoring the highest also require students to display, exhibit, or demonstrate their work in ways that influence an audience beyond school.

SCORE	CRITERIA	NOTES
4	The question, issue, or problem posed by the task requires students to apply Language Arts concepts, literary themes, theories, or issues to clarify, understand, represent, or resolve situations in the world beyond school. The kind of application requested helps students understand the utility of Language Arts in the real world. Students must display, exhibit, or demonstrate their work in ways that will influence an audience beyond school, for example, by communicating what they have learned to others, advocating solutions to social problems, providing assistance to people, creating products, or conducting performances.	
3	The question, issue, or problem posed by the task requires students to apply Language Arts concepts, literary themes, theories, or issues to clarify, understand, represent, or resolve situations in the world beyond school. The kind of application requested helps students understand the utility of Language Arts in the real world. However, there is no effort to use the knowledge to influence an audience beyond school.	
2	The question, issue, or problem posed by the task asks students to apply Language Arts concepts, literary themes, theories, or issues to clarify, understand, represent, or resolve situations in the world beyond school, but the kind of application requested is not likely to help students understand the utility of Language Arts knowledge in the real world.	
1	The task makes little or no demands for students to apply Language Arts concepts, literary themes, theories, or issues to clarify, understand, or resolve situations in the world beyond school.	

Standards and Scoring Criteria for Mathematics Tasks

Standard 1: Construction of Knowledge in Mathematics

The task asks students to organize, interpret, analyze, synthesize, or evaluate information in addressing a mathematical theorem, concept, procedure, or problem, rather than to retrieve or report information as previously given, or to repeatedly apply previously learned algorithms, definitions, rules, and procedures.

Demands for any **ONE** of these cognitive operations (organize, interpret, analyze, synthesize, and evaluate information) signifies an expectation of construction of knowledge because each is a departure from reproducing information as is customary in tasks that ask students only to state previously learned information, algorithms, definitions, rules, and procedures.

A task can be determined to make these demands of students either through explicit written instructions from the teacher (e.g., "Create and solve a multi-step math problem involving measurement, multiplication, and division") or, if instructions are vague, by inferring that the task, even without explicit instructions to organize, interpret, analyze, synthesize, or evaluate information, could be successfully completed **only if** students created a new interpretation or understanding, and not by reproducing an interpretation that they had been given.

Possible indicators of demands for organizing mathematical information include asking students to decide among algorithms, to chart and graph data, or to solve multi-step problems. Possible indicators of mathematical interpretation, synthesis, and evaluation include asking students to consider alternative solutions or strategies for solving mathematical problems, to create their own mathematical problems, or to create a mathematical generalization, pattern, or abstraction from observed data.

SCORE	CRITERIA	NOTES
3	The task's **dominant expectation** is for students to organize, interpret, analyze, synthesize, or evaluate mathematical information rather than merely to reproduce information.	60 – 100% of the time or effort Ⓢ devote to a task
2	There is **some expectation** for students to organize, interpret, analyze, synthesize, or evaluate mathematical information rather than merely to reproduce information.	25 – 60% of Ⓢ time or effort
1	There is **very little or no expectation** for students to organize, interpret, analyze, synthesize, or evaluate mathematical information. The dominant expectation is for students to retrieve or reproduce fragments of knowledge or to repeatedly apply previously learned algorithms, definitions, rules, and procedures.	less than 25% of Ⓢ time or effort

Standard 2: Elaborated Mathematical Communication

The task asks students to express a solution to or conclusions about mathematical concepts, theorems, procedures, or problems **AND** to support their conclusions through coherent explanation or reasoning that involves elaborated use of language (written, oral, or other forms of visual/auditory expression), rather than brief statements.

Possible indicators of demands for elaborated mathematical communication include asking students to generate detailed explanations for their conclusions (e.g., written paragraphs, oral presentations, graphs, tables, equations, diagrams, or sketches).

Through this type of elaborated communication, students are asked to demonstrate understanding of important mathematical concepts, theorems, procedures, or problems. A task that asks for extensive factual or content knowledge alone does not ask for understanding expressed through explanations and supported conclusions.

- What concept are they getting at and what are they concluding about the concept?
- Goes beyond showing their work

SCORE	CRITERIA	NOTES
3	**Full elaboration:** The task asks students to express conclusions about mathematical concepts, theorems, procedures, or problems **AND** to support their conclusions through coherent explanation or reasoning that involves elaborated use of language, and/or diagrams/equations, rather than brief statements.	
2	**Some elaboration:** The task asks students either to express conclusions about mathematical concepts, theorems, procedures, or problems **OR** to offer examples, illustrations, details, or reasons, but not both. The task does not clearly call for both a conclusion and an explanation, reasoning, or details that coherently support the conclusion.	
1	**Little or no elaboration:** The task asks students for little or no elaborated communication about mathematical concepts, theorems, procedures, or problems. The dominant expectation is for short declarative statements, fill-in-the blank, multiple choice, or true-false responses.	

Standard 3: Value Beyond School in Mathematics

The task asks students to use a mathematical concept, theorem, procedure, or problem to clarify, understand, or resolve mathematical situations in the world beyond school.

Consider the extent to which students are asked to apply a mathematical concept, theorem, procedure, or problem, not whether the content or problem posed seems "relevant" to student interests. While "relevance" can increase student engagement, relevance alone doesn't necessarily require student understanding of how mathematics knowledge applies to situations and problems in the real world.

For example, suppose students are asked to design a rectangular playground on a vacant piece of land. The playground's length is to be about 120 feet, the width about 200 feet. The task asks students to describe how they could use the Pythagorean Theorem to make sure the ends are equal in length, the sides are equal in length and all four corners are square (90°). Such a task asks students to use a mathematical theorem and procedures to solve a problem in the world beyond school and helps students understand how academic learning relates to the real world. Tasks scoring the highest also require students to display, exhibit, or demonstrate their work in ways that influence an audience beyond school.

SCORE	CRITERIA	NOTES
4	The question, issue, or problem posed by the task requires students to apply mathematical concepts, theorems, procedures, or problems to clarify, understand, or resolve situations in the world beyond school. The kind of application requested helps students understand the utility of Mathematics in the real world. Students must display, exhibit, or demonstrate their work in ways that will influence an audience beyond school, for example, by communicating what they have learned to others, advocating solutions to problems, providing assistance to people, creating products, or conducting performances.	
3	The question, issue, or problem posed by the task requires students to apply mathematical concepts, theorems, procedures, or problems to clarify, understand, or resolve situations in the world beyond school. The kind of application requested helps students understand the utility of Mathematics in the real world. However, there is no effort to influence an audience beyond school.	
2	The question, issue, or problem posed by the task asks students to apply mathematical concepts, theorems, procedures, or problems to clarify, understand, or explore situations in the world beyond school, but the kind of application requested is not likely to help students understand the utility of Mathematics in the real world.	
1	The task makes little or no demands for students to apply mathematical concepts, theorems, procedures, or problems to clarify, understand, or resolve situations in the world beyond school.	

Standards and Scoring Criteria for Science Tasks

Standard 1: Construction of Knowledge in Science

The task asks students to organize, interpret, analyze, synthesize, or evaluate information in addressing scientific theories, laws, observations, concepts, procedures, or problems, rather than to retrieve or report information as previously given, or to repeatedly apply previously learned procedures.

Demands for any **ONE** of these cognitive operations (organize, interpret, analyze, synthesize, and evaluate information) signifies an expectation of construction of knowledge because each is a departure from reproducing information as is customary in tasks that ask students only to state previously learned information, definitions, rules, and procedures.

Possible indicators of demands for organizing scientific information include asking students to plan and report on experiments, to chart and graph data, or to solve multi-step problems. Possible indicators of scientific interpretation, synthesis, and evaluation include asking students to consider alternative solutions or strategies (decide which formulae or equations to use) for solving scientific problems, to develop scientific hypotheses, to create their own scientific problems, to invent their own solution methods, or to create a scientific generalization, theory, or abstraction from observed data.

A task can be judged to make these demands of students either through explicit written instructions from the teacher (e.g., "Suggest at least two alternative interpretations of why ice forms first on the surface of a body of water, rather than at the bottom") or, if instructions are vague, by inferring that the task, even without explicit instructions to organize, interpret, analyze, synthesize, or evaluate information, could be successfully completed **only if** students created a new interpretation or understanding, and not by reproducing an interpretation that they had been given.

SCORE	CRITERIA	NOTES
3	The task's **dominant expectation** is for students to organize, interpret, analyze, synthesize, or evaluate scientific information, rather than merely to reproduce information, or to repeatedly apply previously learned procedures.	60 - 100% of time or effort ⑤ devote to a task
2	There is **some expectation** for students to organize, interpret, analyze, synthesize, or evaluate scientific information, rather than merely to reproduce information, or to repeatedly apply previously learned procedures.	25 - 60% of ⑤ time or effort
1	There is **very little or no expectation** for students to organize, interpret, analyze, synthesize, or evaluate scientific information. The dominant expectation is for students to retrieve or reproduce fragments of knowledge or to repeatedly apply previously learned procedures.	less than 25% of ⑤ time or effort

Standard 2: Elaborated Scientific Communication

The task asks students to express a conclusion or conclusions about scientific theories, observations, concepts, procedures, or problems **AND** to support their conclusions through coherent explanation or reasoning that involves elaborated use of language (written, oral, or other forms of visual/auditory expression), rather than brief declarations.

Possible indicators of demands for elaborated scientific communication include asking students to generate detailed explanations for their conclusions (e.g., written paragraphs, oral presentations, graphs, tables, equations, diagrams, or sketches).

Through this type of elaborated communication, students are asked to demonstrate understanding of important scientific concepts, theories, or procedures. A task that asks for extensive factual or content knowledge alone does not ask for complex understanding expressed through explanations and supported conclusions.

SCORE	CRITERIA	NOTES
3	**Full elaboration:** The task asks students to express conclusions about a scientific theory, laws, observations, concepts, procedures, or problems **AND** to support their conclusions through coherent explanation or reasoning that involves elaborated use of language, and or diagrams/equations, rather than brief declarations.	
2	**Some elaboration:** The task asks students either to express conclusions about scientific theories, laws, observations, concepts, procedures, or problems **OR** to offer examples, summaries, illustrations, details, or reasons, but not both. The task does not clearly call for both a conclusion and an explanation, reasoning, or details that coherently support the conclusion.	
1	**Little or no elaboration:** The task asks students for little or no elaborated communication about scientific theories, laws, observations, concepts, procedures, or problems. The dominant expectation is for short declarative statements, fill-in-the blank, multiple choice, or true-false responses.	

Standard 3: Value Beyond School in Science

The task asks students to use a scientific concept, theory, law, procedure, or problem to clarify, understand, or resolve scientific situations in the world beyond school.

Consider the extent to which students are asked to apply a scientific concept, theory, law, procedure, or problem, not whether the content or problem posed seems "relevant" to student interests. While "relevance" can increase student engagement, relevance alone doesn't necessarily require student understanding of how science knowledge applies to situations and problems in the real world.

For example, suppose students are asked to design and construct a boat that would float and produce minimum friction as it glides on the surface. The task asks students to analyze buoyancy and resulting differences in friction among the boats. Such a task asks students to use a scientific concept, law, and procedure to solve a scientific problem in the world beyond school and helps students understand how academic learning relates to the real world. Tasks scoring the highest also require students to display, exhibit, or demonstrate their work in ways that influence an audience beyond school.

SCORE	CRITERIA	NOTES
4	The question, issue, or problem posed by the task requires students to apply scientific theories, laws, concepts, procedures, or problems to clarify, understand, or resolve situations in the world beyond school. The kind of application requested helps students understand the utility of Science in the real world. Students must display, exhibit, or demonstrate their work in ways that will influence an audience beyond school, for example, by communicating what they have learned to others, advocating solutions to problems, providing assistance to people, creating products, or conducting performances.	
3	The question, issue, or problem posed by the task requires students to apply scientific theories, laws, concepts, procedures, or problems to clarify, understand, or resolve situations in the world beyond school. The kind of application requested helps students understand the utility of Science in the real world. However, there is no effort to influence an audience beyond school.	
2	The question, issue, or problem posed by the task asks students to apply scientific theories, laws, concepts, procedures, or problems to clarify, understand, or explore situations in the world beyond school, but the kind of application requested is not likely to help students understand the utility of Science in the real world.	
1	The task makes little or no demands for students to apply scientific theories, laws, concepts, procedures, or problems to clarify, understand, or resolve situations in the world beyond school .	

Standards and Scoring Criteria for Social Studies Tasks

Standard 1: Construction of Knowledge in Social Studies

The task asks students to organize, interpret, analyze, synthesize, or evaluate information in addressing Social Studies concepts, themes, theories, observations, procedures, or problems, rather than to retrieve or report information as previously given, or to repeatedly apply previously learned information, definitions, and procedures. Social Studies disciplines include history, economics, political science, geography, sociology, anthropology, psychology, law, as well as applied fields such as criminal justice, medical ethics, etc.

Demands for any **ONE** of these cognitive operations (organize, interpret, analyze, synthesize, and evaluate information) signifies an expectation of construction of knowledge because each is a departure from reproducing information as is customary in tasks that ask students only to state previously learned information, definitions, and procedures.

Possible indicators of demands for organizing Social Studies information include asking students to construct explanations, to chart and graph data, or to summarize historical developments. Possible indicators of Social Studies interpretation, synthesis, and evaluation include asking students to consider alternative perspectives on Social Studies issues, to develop hypotheses to explain social behavior, to evaluate benefits and costs of public policies, to propose ways for citizens to influence public affairs, or to create generalizations from observed data.

A task can be judged to make these demands of students either through explicit written instructions from the teacher (e.g., "What conclusions can you draw from tables showing the number of immigrants to the United States by country of origin between 1890 and 1900?") or, if instructions are vague, by inferring that the task, even without explicit instructions to organize, interpret, analyze, synthesize, or evaluate information, could be successfully completed **only if** students created a new interpretation or understanding, and not by reproducing an interpretation that they had been given.

SCORE	CRITERIA	NOTES
3	The task's **dominant expectation** is for students to organize, interpret, analyze, synthesize, or evaluate Social Studies information, rather than merely to reproduce information, or to repeatedly apply previously learned facts, definitions, and procedures.	60 –100% of time or effort Ⓢ devote to a task
2	There is **some expectation** for students to organize, interpret, analyze, synthesize, or evaluate Social Studies information, rather than merely to reproduce information, or to repeatedly apply previously learned facts, definitions, and procedures.	25–60% of Ⓢ time or effort
1	There is **very little or no expectation** for students to organize, interpret, analyze, synthesize, or evaluate Social Studies information. The dominant expectation is for students to retrieve or reproduce fragments of knowledge, or to repeatedly apply previously learned facts, definitions, and procedures.	less than 25% of Ⓢ time or effort

Standard 2: Elaborated Communication in Social Studies

The task asks students to express a conclusion or conclusions about Social Studies concepts, themes, theories, observations, procedures or problems **AND** to support their conclusions through coherent explanation or reasoning that involves elaborated use of language (written, oral, or other forms of visual/auditory expression), rather than brief declarations.

Possible indicators of demands for elaborated Social Studies communication include asking students to generate detailed explanations for their conclusions (e.g., written explanations and arguments, orally presented position statements, and debates).

Through this type of elaborated communication, students are asked to demonstrate understanding of important Social Studies concepts, themes, theories, or issues. A task that asks for extensive factual or content knowledge alone does not ask for understanding expressed through explanations and supported conclusions.

SCORE	CRITERIA	NOTES
3	**Full elaboration:** The task asks students to express conclusions about Social Studies concepts, themes, theories, observations, procedures, or problems **AND** to support their conclusions through coherent explanation or reasoning that involves elaborated use of language, rather than brief declarations.	
2	**Some elaboration:** The task asks students either to express conclusions about Social Studies concepts, themes, theories, observations, procedures, or problems **OR** to offer examples, illustrations, details, or reasons, but not both. The task does not clearly call for both a conclusion and an explanation, reasoning, or details that coherently support the conclusion.	
1	**Little or no elaboration:** The task asks students for little or no elaborated communication about Social Studies concepts, themes, theories, observations, procedures, or problems. The dominant expectation is for short declarative statements, fill-in-the blank, multiple choice, or true-false responses.	

Standard 3: Value Beyond School in Social Studies

The task asks students to use a Social Studies concept, theme, theory, procedure, or problem to clarify, understand, or resolve situations in the world beyond school.

Consider the extent to which students are asked to apply a Social Studies concept, theme, theory, procedure, or problem, not whether the content or problem posed seems "relevant" to student interests. While "relevance" can increase student engagement, relevance alone doesn't necessarily require student understanding of how social studies knowledge applies to situations and problems in the real world.

For example, suppose students studied the results of civil disobedience in different historical settings and conducted research on social conditions that appear to have maximized the probability of its success. The task asks students to use the results of their research to hypothesize and argue when civil disobedience could be used to foster social change in contemporary situations.

Another task that would score high on this standard would be a task that asked students to investigate the causes of unemployment in their community and to draw conclusions on causes and effects of unemployment using economic, political, or historical concepts. Such a task asks students to use a Social Studies concept, law, or procedure to solve a problem in the world beyond school and helps students understand how academic learning relates to the real world. Tasks scoring the highest also require students to display, exhibit, or demonstrate their work in ways that influence an audience beyond school.

SCORE	CRITERIA	NOTES
4	The question, issue, or problem posed by the task requires students to apply Social Studies concepts, themes, theories, observations, procedures, or problems to clarify, understand, or resolve situations in the world beyond school. The kind of application requested helps students understand the utility of Social Studies in the real world. Students must display, exhibit, or demonstrate their work in ways that will influence an audience beyond school.	
3	The question, issue, or problem posed by the task requires students to apply Social Studies concepts, themes, theories, observations, procedures, or problems to clarify, understand, or resolve situations in the world beyond school. The kind of application requested is credible enough to help students understand the utility of Social Studies knowledge in the real world. However, there is no effort to influence an audience beyond school.	
2	The question, issue, or problem posed by the task asks students to apply Social Studies concepts, themes, theories, observations, procedures, or problems to clarify, understand, or resolve situations in the world beyond school, but the kind of application requested is not likely to help students understand the utility of Social Studies knowledge in the real world.	
1	The task makes little or no demands for students to apply Social Studies topics, theories, observations, concepts, procedures, or problems to clarify, understand, or resolve situations in the world beyond school.	

Standards and Scoring Criteria for Tasks in Any Subject

The research on AIW focused on Language Arts, Mathematics, Science, and Social Studies, but teachers interested in applying the standards to other subjects can use the following standards, criteria, and scoring rules as appropriate for those subjects.

Standard 1: Construction of Knowledge in _____

(specify subject)

The task asks students to organize, interpret, analyze, synthesize, or evaluate information in addressing a concept, procedure, or problem, rather than to retrieve or report information as previously given, or to repeatedly apply previously learned procedures, facts, or definitions.

Demands for any **ONE** of these cognitive operations (organize, interpret, analyze, synthesize, and evaluate information) signifies an expectation of construction of knowledge because each is a departure from reproducing information as is customary in tasks that ask students only to state previously learned information, definitions, rules, and procedures.

Prior to scoring, scorers should attempt to identify and list as part of their scoring guidelines illustrative indicators of task demands for students to organize, interpret, analyze, synthesize, or evaluate information in the subject being scored.

A task can be determined to make these demands of students either through explicit written instructions from the teacher or, if instructions are vague, by inferring that the task, even without explicit instructions to organize, interpret, analyze, synthesize, or evaluate information, could be successfully completed **only if** students created a new interpretation or understanding, and not by reproducing an interpretation that they had been given.

SCORE	CRITERIA	NOTES
3	The task's **dominant expectation** is for students to organize, interpret, analyze, synthesize, or evaluate information in the subject rather than merely to reproduce information, or to repeatedly apply previously learned facts, definitions, and procedures.	60 –100% of time or effort ⑤ devote to a task
2	There is **some expectation** for students to organize, interpret, analyze, synthesize, or evaluate information in the subject rather than merely to reproduce information, or to repeatedly apply previously learned facts, definitions, and procedures.	25 –60% of ⑤ time or effort
1	There is **very little or no expectation** for students to organize, interpret, analyze, synthesize, or evaluate information in the subject. The dominant expectation is for students to retrieve or reproduce fragments of knowledge, or to repeatedly apply previously learned facts, definitions, and procedures.	less than 25% of ⑤ time or effort

Standard 2: Elaborated Communication in _____

(specify subject)

The task asks students to express a conclusion or conclusions about concepts, themes, theories, observations, procedures, or problems **AND** to support their conclusions through coherent explanation or reasoning that involves elaborated use of language (written, oral, or other forms of visual/auditory expression), rather than brief declarations.

Possible indicators of demands for elaborated communication include asking students to generate explanations (e.g., written work, oral presentations, graphs, tables, designs, diagrams, sketches, graphic art, fine art, compositions, structures, or creations). Prior to scoring, scorers should attempt to identify and list as part of their scoring guidelines more specific illustrative indicators of task demands for elaborated communication within the subject.

Through this type of elaborated communication, students are asked to demonstrate understanding of important concepts, themes, theories, or issues. A task that asks for extensive factual or content knowledge alone does not ask for understanding expressed through explanations and supported conclusions.

SCORE	CRITERIA	NOTES
3	**Full elaboration:** The task asks students to express conclusions about concepts, themes, theories, observations, procedures, or problems **AND** to support their conclusions through coherent explanation or reasoning that involves elaborated use of language, rather than brief declarations.	
2	**Some elaboration:** The task asks students either to express conclusions about concepts, themes, theories, observations, procedures, or problems **OR** to offer examples, illustrations, details, or reasons, but not both. The task does not clearly call for both a conclusion and an explanation, reasoning, or details that coherently support the conclusion.	
1	**Little or no elaboration:** The task asks students for little or no elaborated communication about concepts, themes, theories, observations, procedures, or problems. The dominant expectation is for short declarative statements, fill-in-the blank, multiple choice, or true-false responses.	

Standard 3: Value Beyond School in _____

(specify subject)

The task asks students to use the subject's concepts, themes, theories, procedures, or problems to clarify, understand, or resolve situations in the world beyond school.

Consider the extent to which students are asked to apply the subject's concepts, themes, theories, procedures, or problems, not whether the content or problem posed seems "relevant" to student interests. While "relevance" can increase student engagement, relevance alone doesn't necessarily require student understanding of how the knowledge in the subject applies to situations and problems in the real world.

Prior to scoring, scorers should attempt to identify and list as part of their scoring guidelines more specific illustrative indicators of task demands to apply the subject's concepts, themes, theories, procedures, or problems to clarify, understand, or resolve situations in the world beyond school. Examples given for Language Arts, Mathematics, Science, and Social Studies should help to suggest indicators for tasks scoring high on this standard in other subjects as well. Tasks scoring the highest also require students to display, exhibit, or demonstrate their work in ways that influence an audience beyond school.

SCORE	CRITERIA	NOTES
4	The question, issue, or problem posed by the task requires students to apply themes, theories, observations, concepts, procedures, or problems to clarify, understand, or resolve situations in the world beyond school. The kind of application requested helps students understand the utility of the subjects in the real world. Students must display, exhibit, or demonstrate their work in ways that will influence an audience beyond school.	
3	The question, issue, or problem posed by the task requires students to apply themes, theories, observations, concepts, procedures, or problems to clarify, understand, or resolve situations in the world beyond school. The kind of application requested helps students understand the utility of the subject in the real world. However, there is no effort to influence an audience beyond school.	
2	The question, issue, or problem posed by the task asks students to apply concepts, theories, observations, procedures, or problems to clarify, understand, or resolve situations in the world beyond school, but the kind of application requested is not likely to help students understand the utility of the subject in the real world.	
1	The task makes no demands for students to apply the subject's concepts, theories, observations, procedures, or problems to clarify, understand, or resolve situations in the world beyond school.	

Part II
Scoring Student Performance

Introduction and General Rules for Scoring Student Performance

This section presents standards, criteria, and rules for scoring students' authentic intellectual performance in Language Arts, Mathematics, Science, Social Studies, and other subjects. Criteria for assessing students' authentic intellectual work differ from other criteria typically used in grading such as whether students followed teachers' directions, whether they completed all parts of an assignment, whether they demonstrated accurate recall of predefined curriculum content, or whether they demonstrated specific skills. AIW standards, criteria, and scoring rules do not prescribe specific curriculum content or skills for students to master, but AIW standards, criteria, and scoring rules can be used to assess student authentic intellectual work with virtually any curriculum content.

Scores for students' authentic intellectual work need not be used to determine students' grades. Regardless of whether scores on authentic intellectual work are used as part of formal grading, the scoring process alone will help teachers reflect on the kind of learning that should be most valued. Once teachers become comfortable using the AIW standards to design their tasks and lessons and in scoring student performance, they should share the performance standards, criteria, and scoring rules with students and explain the value of assessing students' work this way, in contrast to conventional approaches to assessment. Displaying examples of high scoring authentic student work to the public can demonstrate students' capacities for producing complex and useful intellectual work. Such displays can inspire teachers, students, and the public at large to aspire to intellectual performance of higher quality.

Specific scoring rules will vary somewhat among the subjects, but applying the following **general rules** in all subjects will assist in reaching agreement on student work scores.

1. **Grade Level Expectations.** Take into account what students can reasonably be expected to do at the grade level. After taking grade level expectations into account for each standard, assign scores according to criteria in the standards, not relative to other scores that have been assigned within a grade level group. That is, scores should be based neither on a "curve" within a grade level nor on an assumption that students in earlier grades will score lower than students in later grades.

2. **Selection of Student Work to Score.** During early stages of using the AIW standards, teachers should not attempt to score all students' work according to AIW performance standards, but instead to select samples to score and to discuss with colleagues. The initial purpose of scoring is to help teachers learn the meaning of the standards and how to apply them. There is no one best way to sample student work for this purpose; different sampling rules can be used. A "representative" sample might include high quality, low quality, and average work from the class. An "outlier" sample might focus on what the teacher considers to be the highest-scoring and the lowest-scoring piece of work in the class. A "problematic" sample might include a few pieces of work that the teacher finds most difficult to score. A "student development" sample might include a few pieces of work from one student at different points in time to see if certain trends are evident.

3. **Focus on Scoring Criteria and Evidence in Student Work.** Scores should be based only on evidence in the students' performance relevant to criteria for authentic intellectual work. Since other considerations such as following teachers' directions, completion of all parts of a task, or neatness in presentation are not included in rules for scoring authentic intellectual performance, they should usually be disregarded while scoring on AIW standards. Considerations such as students' linguistic backgrounds and learning disabilities should also be disregarded in assigning AIW scores, although these factors could appropriately influence how students are taught and the conditions under which they complete tasks.

✗ Take the students' names off the work so it doesn't interfere with overall quality of the work (low expectations of certain students for example).

✗ Student work should always bring you back to the task and/or instruction.

4. **Correct Answers and Errors.** High quality authentic intellectual work might contain some inaccuracies or errors, but we would not want to recognize as high quality authentic intellectual performance any piece of student work that contained significant errors.

The main issue for scoring is to determine whether the nature and/or number of errors in the work is significant enough to justify reducing a score that would otherwise be assigned if the errors were not present. This is a matter of professional judgment. The work can first be scored on the relevant standard, under the assumption that there are no significant errors. If it is determined that the nature or quantity of errors is significant enough, then reduce the original score and record the reason for the reduction. No student work should be scored 3 or 4 if significant errors are present.

5. **Translating Descriptive Criteria into Percentages.** Some scoring rules ask the scorer to decide how much of the student's work illustrates the criteria. Scorers who prefer to equate the adjectives we use to percentages can use the following guidelines:

> "Throughout, All, or Almost All" = 80%–100%
> "Moderate or Significant Portion" = 40%–80%
> "Small or Some Portion" = 15%–40%
> "Little or No" = Less Than 15%

6. **Low Scores Due to Low Task Demands.** Scores on student work may be low, not because students were incapable of producing more authentic intellectual work, but because the task failed to call for construction of knowledge, conceptual understanding, or elaborated disciplinary communication. Scores must, nevertheless, be based only on evidence in the student work shown. If scores on student work are consistently low, the teacher should consider revising the task to elevate expectations on AIW standards, revise classroom instruction to better help students improve their performance, or both.

7. **Choosing between Two Close Scores.** When it is difficult to decide between two adjacent scores (4 v. 3, 3 v. 2, or 2 v. 1) use the following rules:

a) If the specific wording of the criteria is not helpful in choosing between two scores, base the score on the general intent or **spirit** of the standard described in the introductory paragraphs of the standard and summarized for each standard below.

Construction of Knowledge: Does student performance demonstrate working with knowledge in the discipline to create generalizations, applications, or interpretations, or does it demonstrate mainly recall and reporting previously received knowledge or repeated application of algorithms?

Conceptual Understanding: Does student performance demonstrate understanding of ideas, concepts, theories, and principles in the discipline by using them to interpret and explain information or solve problems, or does it reveal only superficial and incomplete understanding? (**Note:** If student performance is scored 2 or higher on this standard, the scorer should be able to identify the specific ideas, concepts, theories, and principles in the discipline which appear to be understood by the student.)

Elaborated Communication: Does the student provide a convincing, coherent, and elaborated account of ideas, concepts, theories, and principles in the discipline through extended talk, writing, or other medium, or does student work consist mainly of fragmented statements, lacking in argument and supporting details?

b) Consider the criteria to constitute the *minimum* criteria for each score. Give the higher score only when a persuasive case can be made that the minimum conditions of the higher score have been met. If not, assign the lower score.

Standards and Scoring Criteria for Student Performance in Language Arts

Standard 1: Construction of Knowledge in Language Arts

Student performance demonstrates thinking with Language Arts content by using interpretation, analysis, synthesis, or evaluation to construct knowledge, rather than merely retrieving or restating information given by the teacher or other sources.

Possible indicators of construction of knowledge include students interpreting the significance of key events in a plot or in a character's life, students analyzing the strengths and weaknesses of arguments in a debate, or students creating a "composite" story based both on existing facts and people and on fictional events and characters.

To score high on this standard, the student's work must be original, not merely a restatement of knowledge previously given in a text or discussion.

If the student's work includes only brief answers, without notes, outlines, or other indications of how they arrived at the answers, correct answers alone can indicate construction of knowledge if the scorer concludes that the Language Arts task could be completed successfully **only if** the student had engaged in construction of knowledge.

SCORE	CRITERIA	NOTES
4	**Almost all** of the student's work shows Language Arts interpretation, analysis, synthesis, or evaluation.	80 - 100%
3	A **moderate, yet significant, portion** of the student's work shows Language Arts interpretation, analysis, synthesis, or evaluation.	40 - 80%
2	A **small portion** of the student's work shows Language Arts interpretation, analysis, synthesis, or evaluation.	15 - 40%
1	**Little or none** of the student's work shows Language Arts interpretation, analysis, synthesis, or evaluation.	less than 15%

Standard 2: Conceptual Understanding in Language Arts

Student performance demonstrates understanding of ideas, concepts, theories, and principles in Language Arts by using them to interpret and explain literary passages or works, or other messages—written, spoken, or presented in other ways.

Possible indicators of understanding important Language Arts concepts include expanding upon definitions, representing concepts in alternate ways or contexts, or making connections to other Language Arts concepts, to other disciplines, or to real-world situations.

Correct answers unaccompanied by much explanation can indicate conceptual understanding **if** it is clear that the task or question requires complex conceptual understanding in order to be completed or answered correctly. In this case, the scorer must determine the level of understanding demonstrated and score it appropriately.

In contrast to the standard for construction of knowledge, the score here should be based **not** on the proportion of student work that shows understanding, but on the quality of the understanding wherever it occurs in the work. If student performance is scored 2 or higher on this standard, the scorer should be able to identify the specific ideas, concepts, theories, and principles in the discipline which appear to be understood by the student.

percentage is not the issue
  —where it is and how good it is is the issue

SCORE	CRITERIA	NOTES
4	The student demonstrates exemplary understanding of Language Arts concepts by using them to organize, explain, interpret, summarize, and extend the meaning and significance of otherwise discrete words, passages, or messages.	
3	The student demonstrates significant understanding of Language Arts concepts, but the use of concepts is somewhat limited and/or shows some flaws in understanding.	
2	The student demonstrates some understanding of Language Arts concepts, but shows major limitations in understanding.	
1	The work includes little or no Language Arts concepts, or they are included, but their use shows virtually no conceptual understanding.	

Standard 3: Elaborated Communication in Language Arts

The student provides a convincing, elaborated account of ideas, concepts, theories, and principles in Language Arts through extended writing, talk, or other medium of communication.

To score high, the student should provide:

1) a conclusion, generalization, or argument; and
2) support for it, in the form of examples, illustrations, details, or reasons.
3) In addition, the conclusion should be **coherently linked** to the support. Elaboration is **coherent** when the examples, illustrations, details, or reasons provide appropriate, consistent, and logical support for the conclusions, generalizations, or arguments.

The score should be based **not** on the proportion of student work that contains conclusions and support, but on the quality of the elaborated communication, wherever it may be in the work.

SCORE	CRITERIA	NOTES
4	Elaborated communication is exemplary. Explanations or arguments are clear, complete, accurate, coherent, and convincing, with no significant errors.	
3	Elaboration is offered. Explanations or arguments are reasonably clear and accurate, but lack sufficient support or coherence to be convincing.	
2	Some elaboration is present, but explanations or arguments are noticeably incomplete, contain significant errors, or are incoherent.	
1	Little or no elaboration is offered.	

Standards and Scoring Criteria for Student Performance in Mathematics

Standard 1: Construction of Knowledge in Mathematics

Student performance demonstrates thinking with Mathematics content by using interpretation, analysis, synthesis, or evaluation to construct knowledge, rather than merely retrieving or restating math facts, definitions, and mathematical rules, or repeatedly applying algorithms given by the teacher or other sources.

Possible indicators of mathematical interpretation, analysis, synthesis, or evaluation include students' hypothesizing, describing patterns, making models or simulations, building mathematical arguments, or choosing among or inventing procedures or math problems.

To score high on this standard, the student's work must be original, not merely a restatement of knowledge previously given in a text or discussion.

If the student's work includes only brief answers, but not notes, outlines, computations, or other indications of how they arrived at the answers, correct answers alone can indicate construction of knowledge if the scorer concludes that the mathematical task could be completed successfully **only if** the student had engaged in construction of knowledge.

SCORE	CRITERIA	NOTES
4	Almost all of the student's work shows mathematical interpretation, analysis, synthesis, or evaluation.	80 – 100 %
3	A moderate, yet significant, portion of the student's work shows mathematical interpretation, analysis, synthesis, or evaluation.	40 – 80 %
2	A small portion of the student's work shows mathematical interpretation, analysis, synthesis, or evaluation.	15 – 40 %
1	Little or none of the student's work shows mathematical interpretation, analysis, synthesis, or evaluation.	less than 15%

Standard 2: Conceptual Understanding in Mathematics

Student performance demonstrates understanding of important mathematical concepts by using them to explain numerical information and operations, to create patterns and models, or to solve mathematical problems.

Possible indicators of understanding important mathematical concepts include expanding upon definitions, representing concepts in alternate ways or contexts, or making connections to other mathematical concepts, to other disciplines, or to real-world situations. Correct use of algorithms does not necessarily indicate mathematical conceptual understanding.

If the student's work includes only brief answers, but not notes, outlines, computations, or other indications of how they arrived at the answers, correct answers alone can indicate conceptual understanding **if** the scorer concludes that the mathematical task could be completed successfully. The student must understand the mathematical concept(s) central to the task. In this case, the scorer must determine the level of understanding and score it appropriately. According to this rule, even if students do not show how they arrived at answers, the work may still receive a 3 or 4.

In contrast to the standard for construction of knowledge, the score here should be based **not** on the proportion of student work that shows understanding, but on the quality of the understanding wherever it occurs in the work. If student performance is scored 2 or higher on this standard, the scorer should be able to identify the specific ideas, concepts, theories, and principles in the discipline which appear to be understood by the student.

- different representations of algorithms increase the score

SCORE	CRITERIA	NOTES
4	The student demonstrates exemplary understanding of mathematical concepts by using them to explain numerical information and operations, to create patterns and models, or to solve mathematical problems.	
3	The student demonstrates understanding of the mathematical concepts, but the use of concepts is somewhat limited and/or shows some flaws in understanding.	
2	The student demonstrates some understanding of mathematical concepts, but shows major limitations in understanding.	
1	The work includes little or no mathematical concepts, or they are included, but their use shows virtually no conceptual understanding.	

Standard 3: Elaborated Mathematical Communication

The student provides a convincing, elaborated account of mathematical ideas, concepts, theories, and principles through extended writing, talk, or other medium of communication.

To score high, the student should provide:

1) a conclusion, generalization, or argument; and
2) support for it, in the form of examples, illustrations, details, or reasons.
3) In addition, the conclusion should be **coherently linked** to the support. Elaboration is **coherent** when the examples, illustrations, details, or reasons provide appropriate, consistent, and logical support for the conclusions, generalizations, or arguments.

Consider the extent to which the student presents a clear and convincing explanation or argument. Possible indicators of elaborated mathematical communication include diagrams, drawings, graphs, or symbolic representations (e.g., equations) as well as writing.   (showing their work)

The score should be based **not** on the proportion of student work that contains conclusions and support, but on the quality of the elaborated communication, wherever it may be in the work.

SCORE	CRITERIA	NOTES
4	Elaborated communication is exemplary. Explanations or arguments are clear, complete, accurate, coherent, and convincing, with no significant errors.	
3	Elaboration is offered. Explanations or arguments are reasonably clear and accurate, but lack sufficient support or coherence to be convincing.	
2	Some elaboration is present, but explanations or arguments are noticeably incomplete, contain significant errors, or are incoherent.	
1	Little or no elaboration is offered.	

Standards and Scoring Criteria for Student Performance in Science

Standard 1: Construction of Knowledge in Science

Student performance demonstrates thinking with scientific content by using interpretation, analysis, synthesis, or evaluation to construct knowledge, rather than merely retrieving or restating scientific facts, definitions, and laws, or repeatedly applying procedures given by the teacher or other sources.

Possible indicators of scientific interpretation, analysis, synthesis, or evaluation include students' hypothesizing, describing patterns, making models or simulations, building scientific arguments, or deciding among or inventing procedures.

To score high on this standard, the student's work must be original, not merely a restatement of knowledge previously given in a text or discussion.

If the student's work includes only brief answers, but not notes, outlines, computations, or other indications of how they arrived at the answers, correct answers alone can indicate construction of knowledge if the scorer concludes that the scientific task could be completed successfully **only if** the student had engaged in construction of knowledge. According to this rule, even if students do not show how they arrived at answers, the work may still receive a 3 or 4 for construction of knowledge.

SCORE	CRITERIA	NOTES
4	Almost all of the student's work shows scientific interpretation, analysis, synthesis, or evaluation.	80 – 100 %
3	A moderate, yet significant, portion of the student's work shows scientific interpretation, analysis, synthesis, or evaluation.	40 – 80 %
2	A small portion of the student's work shows scientific interpretation, analysis, synthesis, or evaluation.	15 – 40 %
1	Little or no none of the student's work shows scientific interpretation, analysis, synthesis, or evaluation.	less than 15 %

Standard 2: Conceptual Understanding in Science

Student performance demonstrates understanding of important scientific concepts by using them to explain scientific observations, data, operations, or to solve scientific problems.

Possible indicators of understanding important scientific concepts include identifying patterns, producing models, expanding upon definitions, representing concepts in alternate ways or contexts, or making connections to other scientific concepts, to other disciplines, or to real-world situations. Correct use of scientific methods and procedures does not necessarily indicate understanding of the concepts.

If the student's work includes only brief answers, but not notes, outlines, computations, or other indications of how they arrived at the answers, correct answers alone can indicate conceptual understanding **if** the scorer concludes that the scientific task could be completed successfully. The student must understand the concept(s) relevant to the task. In this case, the scorer must determine the level of understanding and score it appropriately.

In contrast to the standard for construction of knowledge, the score here should be based **not** on the proportion of student work that shows understanding, but on the quality of the understanding wherever it occurs in the work. If student performance is scored 2 or higher on this standard, the scorer should be able to identify the specific ideas, concepts, theories, and principles in the discipline which appear to be understood by the student.

SCORE	CRITERIA	NOTES
4	The student demonstrates exemplary understanding of scientific concepts by using them to explain scientific observations, data, operations, or to solve scientific problems.	
3	The student demonstrates significant understanding of scientific concepts, but the use of concepts is somewhat limited and/or shows some flaws in understanding.	
2	The student demonstrates some understanding of scientific concepts, but shows major limitations in understanding.	
1	The work includes little or no scientific concepts, or they are included, but their use shows virtually no conceptual understanding.	

Standard 3: Elaborated Scientific Communication

The student provides an elaborated account of scientific ideas, concepts, theories, and principles through extended writing, talk, or other medium of communication.

To score high, the student should provide:

1) a conclusion, generalization, or argument; and
2) support for it, in the form of examples, illustrations, details, or reasons.
3) In addition, the conclusion should be **coherently linked** to the support. Elaboration is **coherent** when the examples, illustrations, details, or reasons provide appropriate, consistent, and logical support for the conclusions, generalizations, or arguments.

Consider the extent to which the student presents a clear and convincing explanation or argument. Possible indicators of elaborated scientific communication include diagrams, drawings, graphs, or symbolic representations (e.g., chemical equations) as well as writing.

The score should be based **not** on the proportion of student work that contains conclusions and support, but on the quality of the elaborated communication, wherever it may be in the work.

SCORE	CRITERIA	NOTES
4	Elaborated communication is exemplary. Explanations or arguments are clear, complete, accurate, coherent, and convincing, with no significant errors.	
3	Elaboration is offered. Explanations or arguments are reasonably clear and accurate, but lack sufficient support or coherence to be convincing.	
2	Some elaboration is present, but explanations or arguments are significantly incomplete, contain significant errors, or are incoherent.	
1	Little or no elaboration is offered.	

Standards and Scoring Criteria for Student Performance in Social Studies

Standard 1: Construction of Knowledge in Social Studies

Student performance demonstrates thinking with Social Studies content by using interpretation, analysis, synthesis, or evaluation to construct knowledge, rather than merely retrieving or restating Social Studies facts, concepts, and definitions given by the teacher or other sources.

Possible indicators of Social Studies interpretation, analysis, synthesis, or evaluation include students' hypothesizing, constructing explanations of social events, describing relationships between historical periods and cultures, or making arguments for and against past and contemporary public policies.

To score high on this standard, the student's work must be original, not merely a restatement of knowledge previously given in a text or discussion.

If the student's work includes only brief answers, but not notes, outlines, or other indications of how they arrived at the answers, correct answers alone can indicate construction of knowledge if the scorer concludes that the Social Studies task could be completed successfully **only if** the student had engaged in construction of knowledge. According to this rule, even if students do not show how they arrived at answers, the work may still receive a 3 or 4 for construction of knowledge.

SCORE	CRITERIA	NOTES
4	Almost all of the student's work shows Social Studies interpretation, analysis, synthesis, or evaluation.	80 – 100%
3	A moderate, yet significant, portion of the student's work shows Social Studies interpretation, analysis, synthesis, or evaluation.	40 – 80%
2	A small portion of the student's work shows Social Studies interpretation, analysis, synthesis, or evaluation.	15 – 40%
1	Little or none of the student's work shows Social Studies interpretation, analysis, synthesis, or evaluation.	less than 15%

Standard 2: Conceptual Understanding in Social Studies

Student performance demonstrates understanding of important Social Studies concepts by using them to explain historical and contemporary events, social data and trends, public policies, or to take positions on social issues.

Possible indicators of understanding important Social Studies concepts include identifying patterns in social, political, and economic development, or in human conflict and leadership; expanding upon definitions; representing concepts in alternate ways or contexts; or making connections to other Social Studies concepts, to other disciplines, or to real-world situations. Correct use of Social Studies facts or skills in social inquiry does not necessarily indicate conceptual understanding of the concepts.

If the student's work includes only brief answers, but not notes, outlines, computations, or other indications of how they arrived at the answers, correct answers alone can indicate conceptual understanding **if** the scorer concludes that the Social Studies task could be completed successfully. The student must understand the concept(s) relevant to the task. In this case, the scorer must determine the level of understanding and score it appropriately.

In contrast to the standard for construction of knowledge, the score here should **not** be based on the proportion of student work that shows understanding, but on the quality of the understanding wherever it occurs in the work. If student performance is scored 2 or higher on this standard, the scorer should be able to identify the specific ideas, concepts, theories, and principles in the discipline which appear to be understood by the student.

SCORE	CRITERIA	NOTES
4	The student demonstrates exemplary understanding of Social Studies concepts by using them to explain historical and contemporary events, social data and trends, public policies, or to take positions on social issues.	
3	The student demonstrates significant understanding of Social Studies concepts, but the use of concepts is somewhat limited and/or shows some flaws in understanding.	
2	The student demonstrates some understanding of Social Studies concepts, but shows major limitations in understanding.	
1	The work includes little or no Social Studies concepts, or they are included, but their use shows virtually no conceptual understanding.	

Standard 3: Elaborated Communication in Social Studies

The student provides an elaborated account of Social Studies ideas, concepts, theories, and principles through extended writing, talk, or other medium of communication.

To score high, the student should provide:

1) a conclusion, generalization, or argument; and
2) support for it, in the form of examples, illustrations, details, or reasons.
3) In addition, the conclusion should be **coherently linked** to the support. Elaboration is **coherent** when the examples, illustrations, details, or reasons provide appropriate, consistent, and logical support for the conclusions, generalizations, or arguments.

Consider the extent to which the student presents a clear and convincing explanation or argument. Possible indicators of elaborated Social Studies communication include taking a position on controversial historical claims, social science claims, or public issues and justifying one's position; explaining through prose, drawings, graphs, or photo essays why certain events occurred; or demonstrating how anthropologists, lawyers, or journalists rely on various sources to support their conclusions.

The score should be based **not** on the proportion of student work that contains conclusions and support, but on the quality of the elaborated communication, wherever it may be in the work.

SCORE	CRITERIA	NOTES
4	Elaborated communication is exemplary. Explanations or arguments are clear, complete, accurate, coherent, and convincing, with no significant errors.	
3	Elaboration is offered. Explanations or arguments are reasonably clear and accurate, but lack sufficient support or coherence to be convincing.	
2	Some elaboration is present, but explanations or arguments are significantly incomplete, contain significant errors, or are incoherent.	
1	Little or no elaboration is offered.	

Standards and Scoring Criteria for Student Performance in Any Subject

Standard 1: Construction of Knowledge in _____
(specify subject)

Student performance demonstrates thinking with content in the subject area by using interpretation, analysis, synthesis, or evaluation to construct knowledge, rather than merely retrieving information or restating facts, concepts, and definitions given by the teacher or other sources.

Prior to scoring, scorers should attempt to identify and list as part of their scoring guidelines illustrative indicators of student interpretation, analysis, synthesis, or evaluation in the subject. Indicators for this standard listed for Language Arts, Mathematics, Science, and Social Studies might also be appropriate for other subjects.

To score high on this standard, the student's work must be original, not merely a restatement of knowledge previously given in a text or discussion.

If the student's work includes only brief answers, but not notes, outlines, or other indications of how they arrived at the answers, correct answers alone can indicate construction of knowledge if the scorer concludes that the task could be completed successfully **only if** the student had engaged in construction of knowledge. According to this rule, even if students do not show how they arrived at answers, the work may still receive a 3 or 4 for construction of knowledge.

SCORE	CRITERIA	NOTES
4	Almost all of the student's work shows interpretation, analysis, synthesis, or evaluation.	80 – 100 %
3	A moderate, yet significant, portion of the student's work shows interpretation, analysis, synthesis, or evaluation.	40 – 80 %
2	A small portion of the student's work shows interpretation, analysis, synthesis, or evaluation.	15 – 40 %
1	Little or none of the student's work shows interpretation, analysis, synthesis, or evaluation.	less than 15%

Standard 2: Conceptual Understanding in _____

(specify subject)

Student performance demonstrates understanding of important concepts. Concepts within the subject are represented in ideas, themes, principles, and perspectives that help to explain relationships between more specific forms of information. Approaches to inquiry or expression within a field can also represent important concepts. But correct use of subject specific facts or skills in inquiry does not necessarily indicate conceptual understanding of the concepts.

Possible indicators of understanding important concepts include expanding upon definitions; representing concepts in alternate ways or contexts; or making connections to other concepts, to other disciplines, or to real-world situations. Prior to scoring, scorers should attempt to identify and list as part of their scoring guidelines more specific illustrative indicators of student understanding of important concepts in the subject. Indicators for this standard listed for Language Arts, Mathematics, Science, and Social Studies might also be appropriate for other subjects.

If the student's work includes only brief answers, but not notes, outlines, computations, or other indications of how they arrived at the answers, correct answers alone can indicate conceptual understanding **if** the scorer concludes that the task could be completed successfully. The student must understand the concept(s) relevant to the task. In this case, the scorer must determine the level of understanding and score it appropriately.

In contrast to the standard for construction of knowledge, the score here should **not** be based on the proportion of student work that shows understanding, but on the quality of the understanding wherever it occurs in the work. If student performance is scored 2 or higher on this standard, the scorer should be able to identify the specific ideas, concepts, theories, and principles in the discipline which appear to be understood by the student.

SCORE	CRITERIA	NOTES
4	The student demonstrates exemplary understanding of concepts by using them to explain more specific information, to connect otherwise disparate elements, or to view concrete experiences in a broader perspectives.	
3	The student demonstrates significant understanding of concepts, but their use is somewhat limited and/or shows some flaws in understanding.	
2	The student demonstrates some understanding of concepts, but shows major limitations in understanding.	
1	The work includes little or no concepts, or they are included, but their use shows virtually no conceptual understanding.	

Standard 3: Elaborated Communication in _____

(specify subject)

The student provides a coherent elaborated account of ideas, concepts, theories, and principles through extended writing, talk, or other medium of communication, such as creating a piece of art, writing a musical composition, building a mechanical device, creating a website, or teaching a workout regime to others. The key consideration is the extent to which the elaboration provided is consistent with extended forms of communication in the field being studied.

To score high, the student should provide:

1) a conclusion, generalization, or argument; and
2) support for it, in the form of examples, illustrations, details, or reasons.
3) In addition, the conclusion should be **coherently linked** to the support. Elaboration is **coherent** when the examples, illustrations, details, or reasons provide appropriate, consistent, and logical support for the conclusions, generalizations, or arguments.

Prior to scoring, scorers should attempt to identify and list as part of their scoring guidelines more specific illustrative indicators of student-elaborated communication in the subject. Indicators for this standard listed for Language Arts, Mathematics, Science, and Social Studies might also be appropriate for other subjects.

The score should be based **not** on the proportion of student work that contains conclusions and support, but on the quality of the elaborated communication, wherever it may be in the work.

SCORE	CRITERIA	NOTES
4	Elaborated communication is exemplary. Explanations or arguments are clear, complete, accurate, coherent, and convincing, with no significant errors.	
3	Elaboration is offered. Explanations or arguments are reasonably clear and accurate, but lack sufficient support or coherence to be convincing.	
2	Some elaboration is present, but explanations or arguments are significantly incomplete, contain significant errors, or are incoherent.	
1	Little or no elaboration is offered.	

Standard and Scoring Criteria for Conventions and Usage in Writing

The educational importance of *writing skills* is universally accepted, regardless of whether the *substance* of writing reflects authentic intellectual work. Writing is a critical medium for demonstrating authentic intellectual work. To be sure, authentic intellectual work can be demonstrated in other media, but producing authentic intellectual work in writing is essential because of 1) its many uses in the workplace, in civic life, in personal affairs, and 2) the convenience of using it to facilitate discussions among teachers about the quality of student work. While this standard focuses on conventions and usage in writing independent of the content of a discipline, using it in addition to the discipline-focused elaborated communication standard will enhance assessment of student performance.

This standard is intended to measure the degree to which students successfully use language at the sentence and word level to make their meaning understandable to readers.

Scorers should not count individual errors in grammar, mechanics, sentence structure, and word choice, but instead should assess the degree to which errors interfere with understanding the student's meaning. Scorers should respect student efforts to use language in ways that typically represent a "stretch" for students at their grade level. That is, do not assign significantly lower scores if such "stretch" efforts are not carried off with complete success. As indicated in General Rule #3 (page 36), scorers should assess the quality of the actual written work and not take into consideration possible effects of a student's linguistic background or learning disability on grammar, mechanics, sentence structure, and word choice.

SCORE	CRITERIA	NOTES
4	The student's writing exhibits an **exemplary use** of grammar, mechanics, sentence structure, and word choice. The writing may contain minor errors, but these present no major distractions for the reader.	
3	The student's writing shows **satisfactory and proficient use** of grammar, mechanics, sentence structure, and word choice. There are errors, but they present no problem for understanding the student's meaning.	
2	There are **significant errors** in grammar, mechanics, sentence structure, and word choice. It is difficult but not impossible to understand the student's meaning.	
1	The use of grammar, mechanics, sentence structure, and word choice is **so flawed or limited** that it is not possible to understand the student's meaning.	

Part III
Scoring Instruction

Introduction and General Rules for Scoring Instruction

This section of the manual provides standards, criteria, and scoring rules for assessing the extent to which instruction involves teacher demands for and student participation in authentic intellectual work.

Helping students produce authentic intellectual work requires teachers to think carefully about the kinds of intellectual demands they make on students and the kinds of activities they have students perform during classroom instruction. The AIW framework focuses not on the presence or absence of teaching methods such as lecture, small group discussion, hands-on activities, role-playing simulations, uses of technology, or individual student projects, portfolios, or exhibitions. Instead the focus is on the nature of intellectual work done during class time, regardless of the teaching techniques used.

To determine scores for instruction, follow the descriptions presented for each standard, but also use the following **general rules:**

1. **Grade-Level Expectations.** In scoring the level of AIW in the lesson, take into account what students can reasonably be expected to do at the grade level.

2. **Use Only Evidence Observed During the Lesson.** Base scores only on what is observed during the lesson. Do not score the teacher's plans for the lesson, what students may have done to prepare for the lesson, or what they are likely to do following the lesson.

* Script what you see and hear, not what you think or infer. Base scores on visible evidence.

3. **Evaluating Participation.** Determining how many students participate will be defined as follows:

> **"Almost All" should be interpreted as all but a few of the students.**
> **"Most" refers to more than half of the students.**
> **"Many" refers to at least 1/3 of the students.**
> **"Some" Refers to 10%–30% of the class.**
> **"A Few" should be interpreted as less than 10% of the students.**

4. **Choosing between Two Close Scores.** When it is difficult to decide between two adjacent scores (5 v. 4 or 2 v. 1), use the following rules:

a) If the specific wording of the criteria is not helpful in choosing between two scores, base the score on the general intent or **spirit** of the standard described in the introductory paragraphs of the standard and summarized for each standard below.

- *Higher Order Thinking:* Does the lesson have students work with knowledge in new ways to create generalizations, applications, or interpretations, or does it ask students to recall or reproduce knowledge as it has been given to them?

- *Depth of Knowledge and Student Understanding:* Does the lesson deal with key concepts or themes in ways that develop complex and in-depth student understanding, or does it treat knowledge in superficial, fragmented ways?

- *Substantive Conversation:* Does the lesson use dialogue to build shared and coherent understanding of disciplinary concepts, or does it rely on lecture or short-answer formats to transmit information?

- *Value Beyond School:* Does the lesson have students apply academic knowledge to understand situations and solve problems outside of school, or does it ask students to show academic knowledge only in forms useful to succeed in school?

b) Consider the criteria to constitute the *minimum* criteria for each score. Give the higher score only when a persuasive case can be made that the minimum conditions of the higher score have been met. If not, assign the lower score.

※ HOT and SC standards typically parallel each other — if see a scoring discrepancy between them, you need to take another look.

(T) records a lesson. He/she watches it and then picks the 10-15 minutes that he/she wants the team to watch for whatever reason (i.e., one standard or all the standards).

"Parking lot issue" — something you see in the video that isn't the essence of what you are looking for in terms of evidence for that standard (e.g., boy wearing a baseball cap in the video-taped clssrm).

Standard 1: Higher Order Thinking
(Construction of Knowledge)

- To what extent do students use higher order thinking (HOT) versus lower order thinking (LOT)?

Higher order thinking (HOT) requires students to organize, interpret, analyze, synthesize, or evaluate information about themes, concepts, and problems to draw a conclusion. Scoring is not intended to recognize some of these operations (organize, interpret, synthesize, and evaluate information) as more valued than others. Students demonstrating any **ONE** of these intellectual operations signifies higher order thinking because each is a departure from retrieving, reporting, or reproducing facts, definitions, rules, and procedures, which is often the case in classrooms. In helping students become constructors (not just recipients) of knowledge, instruction for higher order thinking often includes an element of uncertainty because the teacher may not be able to predict what conclusions students will reach.

Lower order thinking (LOT) occurs when students only receive or recite facts, definitions, conventions, or use rules and algorithms repeatedly. As information receivers, students are given pre-specified knowledge conveyed through a reading, worksheet, lecture, or other media. The essence of instruction is to transmit knowledge, to practice procedural routines, or to test students' acquisition and recall of knowledge in forms previously given in texts, lectures, or other messages. Activities that may appear to involve HOT, such as presenting a research project to the class, may actually be dominated by LOT if students only report information that they have retrieved, without having organized or analyzed the information.

- Instruction involves ⑤ in manipulating info and ideas by synthesizing, generalizing, explaining, hypothesizing, or arriving at conclusions that produce new meanings and understandings for them.

Element of uncertainity in HoT → can proceed further but it is of an open-ended nature as not sure what conclusions the ⑤ will reach.

Look at the # of Ⓢ and the types of questions that the teacher is asking.

SCORE	CRITERIA	NOTES
5	Almost all students, almost all of the time, are performing HOT.	All but a few of the Ⓢ HOT
4	There is at least one major activity that occupies a substantial portion of the lesson in which most students perform HOT.	More than 1/2 of the Ⓢ HOT
3	Most students are engaged in LOT for much of the lesson, but there is at least one significant question or activity in which many students perform some HOT.	more than 1/2 of the Ⓢ LOT At least 1/3 of the Ⓢ HOT
2	Most students are engaged in LOT for most of the lesson, but at some point, at least some students perform HOT as a minor diversion within the lesson.	more than 1/2 of the Ⓢ LOT 10-30% of the Ⓢ HOT
1	Most students are engaged only in LOT, i.e., they receive, recite, or participate in routine practice and in no activities during the lesson do students go beyond LOT.	more than 1/2 of the Ⓢ LOT

Evidence: Collect quotes of Ⓣ and/or Ⓢ
- list verbs that are used
- track questions and statements (use tallies)
- what were the questions/statements?
- how often were questions asked?

Did the activity really ask Ⓢ to make new meaning from information?

Standard 2:
Depth of Knowledge and Student Understanding
(Disciplined Inquiry)

To what extent is knowledge deep versus shallow or superficial?

Knowledge is deep when it focuses on a concept, theme, or problem central to an academic, professional, or applied discipline. Deep knowledge reflects complex understandings of these concepts, themes, or problems. This can include understanding relationships, different applications, alternative perspectives/interpretations, and systems that integrate many parts. For students, knowledge is deep when they develop complex understandings of these central concepts. Students can demonstrate systematic, integrated, or holistic understanding when they successfully discover relationships, solve problems, construct explanations, and/or draw conclusions that represent "new" knowledge; that is, new ways for the student to make sense of the world.

Knowledge is shallow, thin, or superficial when 1) it does not deal with a significant concept, theme, or problem central to an academic, professional or applied discipline; or 2) when important, central ideas are oversimplified, presented as non-problematic, or covered in a way that gives students only a superficial acquaintance with their meaning (for example, when teachers present discrete, unconnected ideas and bits of information without explaining their significance or relationships). Shallow understanding is evident when students do not or cannot use knowledge to make clear distinctions, arguments, or solve problems involving concepts, themes, or problems central to an academic, professional, or applied discipline.

Deep knowledge and understanding can be indicated both by the substance of material that the teacher, text, or other medium presents for students to consider during the lesson (AND) by the quality of understanding that students demonstrate as they consider this material. It is possible to have a lesson that contains substantively important, deep knowledge, but in which students do not become engaged or fail to show understanding of the complexity or the significance of the ideas. Observers' ratings can reflect either the depth of the teacher's knowledge or the depth of the understanding that students demonstrate.

* Instruction addresses central ideas of a topic or discipline with enough thoroughness to explore connections and relationships and to produce relatively complex understandings.

Substance of the lesson (concepts, major topics, problem) and the level of understanding that ⓣ and ⓢ have.

Beyond factual knowledge and into conceptual understanding

SCORE	CRITERIA	NOTES
5	Knowledge is very deep. The lesson sustains a focus on a significant disciplinary concept, theme, or problem **AND almost all** students do at least one of the following: demonstrate understanding by arriving at a reasoned explanation or argument of how they answered a question related to a central concept, theme, or problem in a discipline; or demonstrate their understanding of the problematic nature of information and/or ideas central in the discipline. *Has to be the students!*	*All but a few of the ⓢ*
4	Knowledge is relatively deep. The lesson sustains a focus on a significant disciplinary concept, theme, or problem. Either the teacher OR the students provide information, arguments, or reasoning that demonstrates the complexity of an important disciplinary concept, theme, or problem **AND many** students do at least one of the following: demonstrate understanding by arriving at a reasoned explanation or argument of how they answered a question related to a central concept, theme, or problem in a discipline; or demonstrate their understanding of the problematic nature of information and/or ideas central in the discipline.	*At least 1/3 of the ⓢ*
3	Knowledge is treated unevenly during instruction. At least one central concept, theme, or problem is presented in some depth and its significance is grasped by **many** students, but this occupies only a small portion of the lesson. For much of the lesson, some understanding of one central concept, theme, or problem is countered by superficial understanding of other ideas.	*At least 1/3 of the ⓢ*
2	Knowledge remains superficial and fragmented. Some key concepts, themes, or problems are included, but the teacher or students show only a shallow understanding of these.	
1	Knowledge is very thin because it does not deal with central concepts, themes, or problems in the discipline. For most of the lesson, the teacher and students are involved in covering discrete facts, definitions, rules, or procedures.	

Evidence:

- *Listen for the concept and essential question.*
- *Track conceptual statements made by ⓢ and ⓣ*
- *Listen for vocab words that are used correctly*

Evidence:
- *draw exchange lines*
- *draw map of clssrm and keep tailies of who spoke*
- *record # of follow up questions as indicator of exchanges*

Standard 3: Substantive Conversation

(Disciplined Inquiry)

To what extent does classroom talk focus on building shared and coherent understanding of disciplinary concepts through sustained conversation?

This standard measures the extent of talking to learn and understand in the classroom. Classes with high levels of substantive conversation focus on the substance of subject matter and include considerable teacher-student and/or student-student interaction. Substantive conversation has three main features:

1. Talk is about **concepts, themes, and problems in the discipline** and includes higher order thinking such as making distinctions, applying ideas, forming generalizations, or raising questions, not just the reporting of experiences, facts, definitions, or procedures.

2. Conversation involves the **sharing of ideas.** Sharing is best illustrated when participants respond directly to previous speakers by explaining themselves or asking questions to clarify other speakers' statements. Conversation of this sort is not completely scripted or controlled by one party.

3. The dialogue builds on participants' statements to promote a **coherent collective (rather than only individualized) understanding** of a disciplinary concept, theme, or problem. This is illustrated in seminars or small group discussions that, through **sustained conversations**, integrate the contributions of all participants into common understandings shared by the group.

Interchange:
A → B
A ← B

For our purposes, a **sustained conversation** is defined as at least (three consecutive) interchanges between persons in the class. An interchange is a statement by one person and a response by another; this could involve a teacher followed by a student, or a student followed by another student, or a student followed by the teacher. The minimum of three interchanges required for a sustained conversation need not be between the same two people, but whoever participates must respond in ways that build on previous speakers' comments.

To score 2 or above, conversation must involve higher order thinking about concepts, themes, or problems as described above in Feature 1.

- *Students engage in extended conversational exchanges w/ the teacher and/or their peers about subject matter in a way that builds an improved and shared understanding of ideas or topics.*

Need to watch the content and not just who the speakers are

In classes with little or no substantive conversation, interaction typically consists of lectures, explanations, or reports by the teacher or students who deliver pre planned information to the "audience" (students or teacher), whose main task is to listen. The audience might ask questions of the presenter or respond to the presenter's questions, but the goal is to transmit facts or other information, not to use dialogue to build coherent collective understanding.

SCORE	CRITERIA	NOTES
5	Almost all students participate in all three features of substantive conversation, and at least one example of **sustained** conversation occurs.	All but a few of the Ⓢ
4	Most students participate in all three features of substantive conversation, and at least one example of **sustained** conversation occurs.	more than ½ of the Ⓢ
3	Many students participate in Feature 2 (sharing) **AND/OR** Feature 3 (coherent collective understanding) of substantive conversation, and at least one example of **sustained** conversation occurs.	At least ⅓ of the Ⓢ
2	Some students participate in either Feature 2 (sharing) **OR** Feature 3 (coherent collective understanding). *Must have HOT*	10-30% of the Ⓢ
1	Virtually no features of substantive conversation occur, or only a few students participate in features that do occur.	less than 10% of the Ⓢ

* *Whole group will generally score lower here because it almost always inhibits all Ⓢ from participating.*

** *Teacher can be one of the exchanges, but it is not teacher-directed or controlled interchanges.*

Evidence:
- *listen for concept and methods or processes in the discipline as they relate to real word application*
- *record when connections occur and who is making the connection*

Standard 4: Value Beyond School

(Connections to the World Beyond the Classroom)

- To what extent does instruction help students use knowledge in academic disciplines to address situations, issues, and problems in the world beyond school?

Authentic intellectual work employs knowledge, concepts, or processes used within academic, professional, or applied disciplines to understand situations and solve problems in contexts beyond school. Such issues and problems might relate to civic life, workplace experience, or personal affairs (e.g., experiences within the family, as a consumer, or during leisure time) that students have encountered or are likely to encounter in their lives beyond school. When intellectual work in the classroom helps students to address and understand situations and problems beyond the classroom, we assume the work they do in class has value and meaning for them beyond the benefits of achieving success in school.

Intellectual work useful for answering questions, performing tasks, and solving problems posed only in the school context is less authentic because it serves only to certify students' level of competence or compliance with the norms and routines of formal schooling, offering no assurance that students' knowledge or skills will have value and meaning in the world beyond school.

SCORE	CRITERIA	NOTES
5	Most students use knowledge or skills of an academic, professional, or applied discipline to study or work on a concept, theme, or problem in contexts beyond school. The students recognize the value of classroom knowledge/skills in understanding or addressing situations outside the classroom. They also apply their knowledge and skills to influence an audience beyond their classroom; for example, by communicating what they have learned to others, advocating solutions to social problems, providing assistance to people, creating products, or conducting performances that others will value.	*more than ½ of the ⑤* *Not the physical location; can also bring the community to the school.* *Not a generic audience; has a focused or linked purpose.*

↓
btwn the audience and content

- *Students make connections btwn substantive knowledge and either public problems or personal experiences.*

(VBS)

a) addressing an actual problem of some contemporary significance
b) building on students' personal experiences to teach impt. ideas in the disciplines
c) students communicate their knowledge to others beyond the classroom in ways that assist or influence others

SCORE	CRITERIA	NOTES
4	Most students use knowledge or skills of an academic, professional, or applied discipline to study or work on a concept, theme, or problem in contexts beyond school. The students recognize the value of classroom knowledge/skills in understanding or addressing situations outside the classroom. However, there is no effort to use the knowledge to influence an audience beyond the classroom.	more than 1/2 of the (S)
3	Many students use knowledge or skills of an academic, professional, or applied discipline to study or work on a concept, theme, or problem in contexts beyond school. But only some of these students recognize the value of classroom knowledge/skills in understanding or addressing situations outside the classroom.	At least 1/3 of the (S) 10 - 30% of the (S)
2	Some students use knowledge or skills of an academic, professional, or applied discipline to study or work on a concept, theme, or problem in contexts beyond school. These students may or may not recognize the value of classroom knowledge/skills in understanding or addressing situations outside the classroom.	10 - 30% of the (S)
1	There is no connection between the lesson and contexts beyond school. Knowledge or skills of an academic, professional, or applied discipline are not used to study or work on a concept, theme, or problem in contexts beyond school. The teacher may try to explain connections between academic learning and problems in non-school contexts (e.g., the teacher might inform students that understanding Middle Eastern history is important for understanding the price of gasoline and oil in the U.S.), but students are not involved in applying such knowledge, nor do they recognize the value of classroom knowledge/skills in understanding or addressing situations outside the classroom.	

What is the context the teacher is using for them to work with the content and/or concept?

Evidence that students see the connection